skin divers

skin divers

ANNE MICHAELS

BLOOMSBURY

First published in Great Britain 1999

Copyright © 1999 by Anne Michaels

The moral right of the author
has been asserted

Bloomsbury Publishing Plc,
38 Soho Square, London W1V 5DF

A CIP catalogue record for this book
is available from the British Library

ISBN 0 7475 4453 0

10 9 8 7 6 5 4 3 2 1

Printed in Great Britain by
St Edmundsbury Press, Suffolk

CONTENTS

I.

Three Weeks   3
Skin Divers   4
Land in Sight   9
Night Garden   11
Into Arrival   13
Wild Horses   15
There Is No City That Does Not Dream   16
Last Night's Moon   17
The Passionate World   26

II.

The Second Search   31
Ice House   37
The Hooded Hawk   43

III.

Fontanelles   51

A Note on the Text   65
Acknowledgements   67

skin divers

I

THREE WEEKS

Three weeks longing, water burning
stone. Three weeks leopard blood
pacing under the loud insomnia of stars.
Three weeks voltaic. Weeks of winter
afternoons, darkness half descended.
Howling at distance, ocean
pulling between us, bending time.
Three weeks finding you in me in new places,
luminescent as a tetra in depths,
its neon trail.
Three weeks shipwrecked on this mad island;
twisting aurora of perfumes. Every boundary of body
electrified, every thought hunted down
by memory of touch. Three weeks of open eyes
when you call, your first question,
Did I wake you . . .

Under the big-top
of stars, cows drift
from enclosures, bellies brushing
the high grass, ready for their heavy
festivities. Lowland gleams like mica
in the rain. Starlight
soaks our shoes.
The seaweed field begs, the same
burlap field that in winter cracks with frost,
is splashed by the black brush
of crows. Frozen sparklers of Queen Anne's lace.

Because the moon feels loved, she lets our eyes
follow her across the field, stepping
from her clothes, strewn silk
glinting in furrows. Feeling loved, the moon loves
to be looked at, swimming
all night across the river.

She calls through screens,
she fingers a white slip in the night hallway,
reaches across the table for a glass.
She holds the dream fort.
Like the moon, I want to touch places

just by looking. To tell
new things at three in the morning, when we're
awake with rain or any sadness, or slendering through
reeds of sleep, surfacing to skin. In this room
where so much has happened, where love
is the clink of buttons as your shirt slides
to the floor, the rolling sound of loose change;
a book half open, clothes
half open. Again we feel
how transparent the envelope
of the body, pushed through the door
of the world. To read what's inside
we hold each other
up to the light. We hold
the ones we love or long
to be free of, carry them
into every night field, sit with them
while cows slow as ships
barely move in the distance.
Rain dripping from the awning of stars.

Waterworn, the body remembers
like a floodplain, sentiment-laden,
reclaims itself with every tide.
Memory terraces, soft as green deltas.
Or reefs and cordilleras —
gathering the world to bone.

The moon touches everything
into meaning, under her blind fingers,
then returns us to cerulean
aluminum dawns. Night,
a road pointing east.
Her sister, memory, browses the closet
for clothes carrying someone's shape.
She wipes her hands on an apron
stained with childhood, familiar smells
in her hair; rattles pots and pans
in the circadian kitchen.
While in the bedroom of a night field,
the moon undresses; her abandoned peignoir
floats forever down.

Memory drags possessions out on the lawn,
moves slowly through wet grass, weighed down
by moments caught in her night net, in the glistening
ether of her skirt. The air alive,
memory lifts her head and I nearly
disappear. You lift your head, a look I feel
everywhere, a tongue of a glance,
and love's this dark field, our shadow web
of voices, the carbon-paper purple
rainy dark. Memory's heavy with the jewellery
of rain, her skirt heavy with buds of mercury

congealing to ice on embroidered branches —
as she walks we hear the clacking surf
of those beautiful bones. Already love
so far beyond the body, reached only
by way of the body. Time is the alembic
that turns what we know
into mystery. Into air,
into the purple stain of sweetness.
Laburnum, wild iris, birch forest so thick
it glows at night, smells that reach us
everywhere; the alchemy that keeps us
happy on the ground, even if our arms embrace
nothing, nothing: the withdrawing
trochee of birds. We'll never achieve escape
velocity, might as well sink into wet
firmament, learn to stay under,
breathing through our skin.
In silver lamella, in rivers
the colour of rain. Under water, under sky;
with transparent ancient wings.

Tonight the moon traipses in bare feet,
silk stockings left behind
like pieces of river.

Our legs and arms, summer-steeped,

slapped damp
with mud and weeds.

We roll over the edge into the deep field,
rise from under rain,
from our shapes in wet grass.
Night swimmers, skin divers.

All day the sky
whispered into the sea and the sails
would not fill. On the pier,
dogs drank the air dry
with searching tongues.
We were seared wherever clothes
revealed us. Down the boulevard,
shutters clapped loud against the sun.
Children slipped messages through the slats,
flecks of paper drifted into the street.

All through the city love looked for us, through
the crooked *Altestrasse*, under Lenin's balcony,
past the terrace where Goethe drank his coffee.
Into cafés where coolness turns its key
in a shadow. All day love followed us
as we climbed, from fountain to bridge.
A gull hovered as if
broken. All day love drew its finger
across my belly, ascended my damp spine.
I kept turning my face
from its breath.

The city woke. Dogs unfolded their legs
and stood. One by one, shutters parted,

glimpses of voices
pressed the air.

The same loneliness that closes us
opens us again.

Like hair loosened by the sea,
slowly the darkness opens into darkness.

NIGHT GARDEN

Your mouth, a hand
against my mouth.
Pressed to earth, we dream
of ocean: heat-soaked, washed
with exhaustion, our mariner's sleep
haunted by smells of garden – fresh rosemary
thirty miles off Spain. Long grasses
sway the bottom of our boat.
We follow a sequence
of scents complex as music,
navigate earth places, sea places, follow
acoustics of mountains,
warbler instinct in the dark –
Siberia, Africa, and back –
phosphor runways guiding us to shore,
moonlight half eaten by the waves.

Across the lawn, a lit window floats.
Welts of lupine. You remember
an open window, Arabian music
through wet beeches. We know we're moving
at tremendous speed, that if it could be seen
the stars would be a smear
of velocity. But all is still,

pinioned. In the night garden,
light is a swallowed cry.
Naked in the middle of the city
the stars grow firm in our mouths.

INTO ARRIVAL

It will be in a station
with a glass roof
grimy with the soot
of every train and
they will embrace for every mile
of arrival. They will not
let go, not all the long way,
his arm in the curve
of her longing. Walking in a city
neither knows too well,
watching women with satchels
give coins to a priest for the war veterans;
finding the keyhole view of the church
from an old wall across the city, the dome
filling the keyhole precisely,
like an eye. In the home
of winter, under an earth
of blankets, he warms her skin
as she climbs in from the air.

There is a way our bodies
are not our own, and when he finds her
there is room at last
for everyone they love,

the place he finds,
she finds, each word of skin
a decision.

There is earth
that never leaves your hands,
rain that never leaves
your bones. Words so old they are broken
from us, because they can only be
broken. They will not
let go, because some love
is broken from love,
like stones
from stone,
rain from rain,
like the sea
from the sea.

WILD HORSES

Minarets of burdock
clang in the copper marsh, the grapes'
frozen skins flood with sweetness.
Winter trees burned to black wicks.

Harnessed, longing cuts
with every turn. Time has one direction,
to divide. Invisible, it casts shadow
canyons, tools furrows into leather fields,
carves oxbow rivers of birds
into cold November skies.

Then, the first stars' faint static,
the sacred transmissions, the hair's
breadth of the intimate
infinite. Iron-oxide sun stains travertine sky,
sudden colour like the ochre
horses of Dordogne, stampeding into lamplight.
Liquid grasses overflow like dark ale.
Twilight is a cave, pungent
with wet hides, torches of resin.

Under the pulling moon, the strap of river
digs into the flesh of field.

There is no city that does not dream
from its foundations. The lost lake
crumbling in the hands of brickmakers,
the floor of the ravine where light lies broken
with the memory of rivers. All the winters
stored in that geologic
garden. Dinosaurs sleep in the subway
at Bloor and Shaw, a bed of bones
under the rumbling track. The storm
that lit the city with the voltage
of spring, when we were eighteen
on the clean earth. The ferry ride in the rain,
wind wet with wedding music and everything that
sings in the carbon of stone and bone
like a page of love, wind-lost from a hand, unread.

LAST NIGHT'S MOON

"When will we next walk together
under last night's moon?"
— Tu Fu

March aspens, mist
forest. Green rain pins down
the sea, early evening
cyanotype. Silver saltlines, weedy
toques of low tide, pillow lava's
black spill indelible
in the sand. Unbroken
broken sea.

←

Rain sharpens marsh-hair
birth-green of the spring firs.
In the bog where the dead never disappear,
where river birch drown, the surface
strewn with reflection. This is the acid-soaked
moss that eats bones, keeps flesh;
the fermented ground where time stops and
doesn't; dissolves the skull, preserves
the brain, wrinkled pearl in black mud.

←

In the autumn that made love
necessary, we stood in rubber boots
on the sphagnum raft and learned
love is soil – stronger than peat or sea –
melting what it holds.

The past
is not our own. Mole's ribbon of earth,
termite house,
soaked sponge. It rises,
keloids of rain on wood; spreads,
milkweed galaxy, broken pod
scattering the debris of attention.
Where you are
while your body is here, remembering
in the cold spring afternoon.

The past
is a long bone.

←

Time is like the painter's lie, no line
around apple or along thigh, though the apple
aches to its sweet edge, strains

to its skin, the seam
of density. Invisible line
closest to touch. Line of wet grass
on my arm, your tongue's
wet line across my back.

All the history in the bone-embedded hills
of your body. Everything your mouth
remembers. Your hands manipulate
in the darkness, silver bromide
of desire darkening skin with light.

↤

Disoriented at great depths,
confused by the noise of shipping routes,
whales hover, small eyes squinting as they consult
the magnetic map of the ocean floor. They strain,
a thousand miles through cold channels;
clicking thrums of distant loneliness
bounce off seamounts and abyssal plains. They look up
from perpetual dusk to rods of sunlight,
a solar forest at the surface.

Transfixed in the dark summer
kitchen: feet bare on humid
linoleum, cilia listening. Feral

as the infrared aura of the snake's prey, the bees'
pointillism, the infrasonic
hum of the desert heard by birds.

The nighthawk spans the ceiling;
swoops. Hot kitchen air
vibrates. I look up
to the pattern of stars under its wings.

↙

If love wants you; if you've been melted
down to stars, you will love
with lungs and gills, with warm blood
and cold. With feathers and scales.
Under the hot gloom of the forest canopy
you'll want to breathe with the spiral
calls of birds, while your lashing tail
still gropes for the waves. You'll try
to haul your weight from simple sea
to gravity of land. Caught by the tide,
in the snail-slip of your own path, for moments
suffocating in both water and air.
If love wants you, suddenly your past is
obsolete science. Old maps,
disproved theories, a diorama.

The moment our bodies are set to spring open.
The immanence that reassembles matter
passes through us then disperses
into time and place:
the spasm of fur stroked upright; shocked electrons.
The mother who hears her child crying upstairs
and suddenly feels her dress
wet with milk.
Among black branches, oyster-coloured fog
tongues every corner of loneliness we never knew
before we were loved there,
the places left fallow when we're born,
waiting for experience to find its way
into us. The night crossing, on deck
in the dark car. On the beach where
night reshaped your face.
In the lava fields, carbon turned to carpet,
moss like velvet spread over splintered forms.

The instant spray freezes
in air above the falls, a gasp of ice.
We rise, hearing our names
called home through salmon-blue dusk, the royal moon
an escutcheon on the shield of sky.
The current that passes through us, radio waves,
electric lick. The billions of photons that pass
through film emulsion every second, the single

submicroscopic crystal struck
that becomes the photograph.
We look and suddenly the world
looks back.
A jagged tube of ions pins us to the sky.

↤

But if, like starlings, we continue to navigate
by the rear-view mirror
of the moon; if we continue to reach
both for salt and for the sweet white
nibs of grass growing closest to earth;
if, in the autumn bog red with sedge we're also
driving through the canyon at night,
all around us the hidden glow of limestone
erased by darkness; if still we wish
we'd waited for morning,
we will know ourselves
nowhere.
Not in the mirrors of waves
or in the corrading stream,
not in the wavering
glass of an apartment building,
not in the looming light of night lobbies
or on the rainy deck. Not in the autumn kitchen
or in the motel where we watched meteors

from our bed while your slow film, the shutter open,
turned stars to rain.

We will become
indigestible. Afraid
of choking on fur
and armour, animals
will refuse the divided longings
in our foreign blue flesh.

←

In your hands, all you've lost,
all you've touched.
In the angle of your head,
every vow and
broken vow. In your skin,
every time you were disregarded,
every time you were received.
Sundered, drowsed. A seeded field,
mossy cleft, tidal pool, milky stem.
The branch that's released when the bird lifts
or lands. In a summer kitchen.
On a white winter morning, sunlight across the bed.

←

Try to keep everything and keep
standing. In the tall grass,
ten thousand shadows. What's past,
all you've been,
will continue its half-life,
a carbon burn searing its way to heaven
through the twisted core of a pine.
At night, memory will roam your skin.
Your dreams will reveal the squirming world
under the lifted stone.
While you sleep, the sea
floods your house, you wake
to silt, long brown weeds
tangled in the sheets. You wake
in the bog, caked with the froth of peat,
stunted as shore pine,
growing a metre a century.

The bog bruised with colour,
muskeg, hardpan, muck.
Matted green sphagnum
thick as buffalo fur.
Sinking into, buoyed
by spongy ground;
walking on water.

In time, night after night,
we'll begin to dream of a langsam sea,
waves in slow motion, thickening to sand.
Drenched with satiety we'll be slow
to rise, a metre a century.

Our brown bed is peat,
born of water, flooded,
burning with the smell of earth.

is round. For days we sail, for months,
and still the way is new; strange stars.
Drawn to you, taut over time,
ropes connect this floating floor
to the wind, fraying into sound.

To arrive is to sleep
where we stop moving.
Past the shoal of clothes
to that shore, heaped with debris
of words. A hem of salt,
white lace, on sea-heavy legs.

Love longs for land. All night
we dream the jungle's sleepy electricity;
gnashing chords of insects swim in our ears
and we go under, into green. All night
love draws its heavy drape of scent against the sea
and we wake with the allure of earth in our lungs,
hungry for bread and oranges.
Salamanders dart from your step's shadow, disappear
among wild coffee, fleshy cacti, thorny succulents and
flowers like bowls to save the rain.
We are sailors who wake when the moon intrudes

the smoky tavern of dreams, wake to find a name on an arm
or our bodies bruised by sun or the pressure of a hand,
wake with the map of night on our skin,
traced like moss-stained stone.

Lost, past the last familiar outpost,
flat on deck, milky light cool on our damp hair,
we look up past the ship's angles to stars austere
as a woodcut, and pray we never reach
the lights of that invisible city, where,

landlocked, they have given up on our return.
But some nights, woken by wind,
looking up at different stars,
they are reminded of us, the faint taste of
salt on their lips.

II

THE SECOND SEARCH

"Yesterday at the cemetery, I did not succeed in understanding
the words 'Pierre Curie' engraved on the stone."
— Marie Curie, 1906

The truth likes to hide
out in the open. Even then,
alone on the bridge, in the solitude
of desire, our moon flooded
the gorges of Truyère. Even then
the satin muscle of a melody
twisted over water, waiting
to be heard: over the Wisła, the Bièvre,
the Seine. Rain tugged with invisible hands
on cedar beards, dug into riverbanks,
squeezed the smell of earth in its fists —
as if it knew someday I'd reach
into powdery brown ore
flecked with needles of Bohemian pines,
stand forty-five months under umbrellas or wet
under sun, stirring the blue spirit
from the bitter breath of pitchblende.
So much to burn through, years, to reach
that colour. As if Polish rain already knew
our flooded garden in Paris: I waited

while you were carried
home from Rue Dauphine, half your skull
hardened into pavement; moonlight's blade
against the throats of flowers, pink flesh
soaked, purple mouths open,
shouts turned to dust on their tongues.
Sepia damp like the forests of Minière and Port Royale
you'd described, guiding me to sleep: even then
instructing me not to fear
the ground, to give thanks
to the worm-churned paths
of failure that brought us together,
to refuse the shroud, cover you instead
with hawthorne, iris, the black cloth
of earth you loved.

Before we married
I stood above the river
pulling at my hands
as if I'd already lost something so beautiful
my skin was stained. How similar
the leap of faith and the leap
of fear. While a bird
signed its name on the sky. Even then
I felt you through my clothes, like the radium kiss
through Becquerel's vest pocket, the kiss he never forgot,
burning into his belly.

I pulled apart your coat
looking for you. I kissed your cloth shadow and kept
your blood under my nails. I screamed at Irène
for closing a book you'd left open on a table.

The longer we lived together, the more
I loved you. Day after day
I poured something purer
into basins and jars. I watched you
bent over your table like a jeweller,
setting things that can't be seen. The joy
of concentration, the elements
love precipitates to. By then our hands
never stopped moving, our skin
was wool, long gloves eating us
to the bone. We opened the door to
the aurora borealis, to icebergs, to distant
mountains lining the shelves.
The blue residue that clings like scent,
fogs everything with its breath.
At night, at work, we sat as if
under stars. The glowing distillation
of time.

You laughed when I marked cookbooks
with the same care as notes in the lab

but for me it was the same: the same
details of love – dissolving, filtering, collecting
until truth is so small it fits
on the tongue. My body sore from standing
in the yard, stirring. Or from stretching
under you.
Night sounds on the lawn
at Sceaux, lamps on the porch,
wooden legs scraping flagstones
as your father followed the moon with his chair.
Listening to a song on dark drifts over the river
knowing there was no difference, your hand
asleep on my side, whether you were thinking
of essential salts or atomic numbers or the secret
effects of moonlight: it was the same love,
radiant with memory, simple as skin.

Everything we touch
burns away, whether we give ourselves
or not, the same April day spreads to thinness,
the same winter afternoon
thickens to dark. I was thirty-eight years old.
Every time a door opened
I expected you. For months I hid your clothes
stiff with blood.
Only the street understood. I walked

and shut my eyes, gave myself up to the God
of trams, horses, cabs.

You are the glass that silences
wet leaves, the silence of the winter river.
I no longer see the world
with your eyes, but see you
in the world: invisibility bending the branch;
the moon wobbling, just halved;
skin vanishing under the rays.
When Albert in the middle of a proof
suddenly slung off his rucksack
to stare down the chasms of Engandine,
grabbing my arm, wild: "I need to know
what happens to passengers
when the elevator falls into emptiness" —
and I held our girls, afraid
they'd laugh themselves over the edge —
it was you I'd been thinking of,
as we crossed the Majola Pass.

I take our daughters
to the rivers you loved.
We walk along the Bièvre
where you spent whole nights
fishing ideas out of the water.
I think of silver skin,

invisible in the current, yet
separating cold bright blood
from the colourless river. Invisible
as oxygen sealing water and ice,
so the line between river and sky
won't break, hydrogen aligning itself
in one direction, under skaters' blades.
Moving faster with each slow stride.
Nothing warms like motion,
speed in our thighs.

I can only find you
by looking deeper, that's how love
leads us into the world.

My hands burn
all the time.

ICE HOUSE

"I regret nothing but his suffering."
— Kathleen Scott

Wherever we cry,
it's far from home.

←

At Sandwich, our son pointed
persistently to sea.
I followed his infant gaze,
expecting a bird or a boat
but there was nothing.
How unnerving,
as if he could see you
on the horizon,
knew where you were
exactly:
at the edge of the world.

←

You unloaded the ship at Lyttleton
and repacked her:

"thirty-five dogs
five tons of dog food
fifteen ponies
thirty-two tons of pony fodder
three motor-sledges
four hundred and sixty tons of coal
collapsible huts
an acetylene plant
thirty-five thousand cigars
one guinea pig
one fantail pigeon
three rabbits
one cat with its own hammock, blanket and pillow
one hundred and sixty-two carcasses of mutton and
an ice house"

&

Men returned from war
without faces, with noses lost
discretely as antique statues,
accurately as if eaten
by frostbite.
In clay I shaped their

flesh, sometimes
retrieving a likeness
from photographs.
Then the surgeons copied
nose, ears, jaw
with molten wax and metal plates
and horsehair stitches;
with borrowed cartilage,
from the soldiers' own ribs,
leftovers stored under the skin
of the abdomen. I held the men down
until the morphia
slid into them.
I was only sick
afterwards.

Working the clay, I remembered
mornings in Rodin's studio,
his drawerfuls of tiny hands and feet,
like a mechanic's tool box.
I imagined my mother in her blindness
before she died, touching my face,
as if still she could
build me with her body.

At night, in the studio
I took your face in my hands and your fine

arms and long legs, your small waist,
and loved you into stone.

The men returned from France
to Ellerman's Hospital.
Their courage
was beautiful.
I understood the work at once:
To use scar tissue to advantage.
To construct through art,
one's face to the world.
Sculpt what's missing.

＋

You reached furthest south,
then you went further.

In neither of those forsaken places
did you forsake us.

＋

At Lyttleton the hills unrolled,
a Japanese scroll painting;
we opened the landscape with our bare feet.

So much learned by observation.
We took in brainfuls of New Zealand air
on the blue climb over the falls.

Our last night together we slept
not in the big house but
in the Kinseys' garden.
Belonging only
to each other.
Guests of the earth.

←

Mid-sea, a month out of range
of the wireless;
on my way to you. Floating
between landfalls,
between one hemisphere and another.
Between the words
"wife" and "widow."

←

Newspapers, politicians
scavenged your journals.

But your words
never lost their way.

←

We mourn in a place no one knows;
it's right that our grief be unseen.

I love you as if you'll return
after years of absence.
As if we'd invented
moonlight.

←

Still I dream
of your arrival.

THE HOODED HAWK

for A.W.

"... I had come into my own; painful to the extreme limit
of endurance as that place and state might be."
— Kathleen Raine

History chokes on the little bones
of meaning, the little bones
of love. Early winter, late
afternoon, the room went dark.
We sat a long time
before noticing. You were recounting
a trip to Rome, not the conference
but a woman who remembered those who hid
or fled. You stood to turn on a lamp, instead
sat down again. Your voice
more distinct in darkness.

You knew it like a secret:
the chalk body outlined
under the skin, "the line," you wrote,
between "what's permissible" and "what's
possible." History: the silver spoon
in your kitchen drawer,
swastika on its handle. The "tulips and daffodils"
escaping children were told to run to, who

remember instead "bloodhounds and rats."
Your mother's dolls — all the refugee parts
we're made of. History is the love that enters us
through death; its discipline
is grief. You never forgot the floating ghettos:
landlocked in north Winnipeg, listening with your father
to the radio, while the boat was refused
at every port. Eleven years old,
you were with them, those who had no place,
while the streetcars squealed to a turn
on North Main, and in the front room
the sewing machines and wooden steaming blocks
thudded all night; with them
listening to your mother tell of her
escape across the river —
"we must bring our children to a shore";
and again in '55, alone on deck,
anxious to begin as a writer;
with them when we spoke of
exiled Walter Benjamin, who devoured books
"the way a flame 'reads' wood,"
or when later you wrote of your childhood:
"I belonged where I read."

The dolls your mother made
were stories. "He's the French type . . .
dresses just so . . . he likes to chase after women . . ."
She holds up an Englishman and in her other hand
his pregnant wife: "Now he's more mature
for his responsibilities." When the stories were sad
she dressed them in finery
so we wouldn't turn away. After a pogrom, when she was young,
your mother rooted out buttons and bits of glass,
"scraps of this and that" and never stopped: wooden spools,
used light bulbs, leftover leather, bottle tops,
lids of jars, labels, beads,
bone. Her one requirement: that the object
had lost its purpose. So what was torn
transformed to something whole:
a hat, a foot, a hand.
Your mother sewed all night
and fell asleep on the cutting table.

All your writing life, you worked at night.

One Thanksgiving it took two
to carry the platter — your idea,
a cauliflower steamed whole,

cerebral and surreal, regal
as the head of a saint. Elevated
to a centrepiece. I understood the symbol:
they harvested cauliflowers
from the fields near Terezin . . .
At the table, your favourite ghost sat with us,
the poet, Heine, who knew home
is in the mouth: not just language but
carp in raisin sauce, lamb
with horseradish and garlic —
even in Paris, surrounded by *cuisine*.

    ↤

In your unlit apartment.
After another stage of illness.
All the years were with us.

Of your mother's death
you wrote, "My loss is endless . . . its only closure
will be my own." This winter afternoon, two years after
your death, sorrow magnifies
through the generations, each human's part
heaped upon the next, in this way our griefs
are joined. For all the talk,
for all the speaking up and
out, the core sample

is silence. We made a pact
of dusk. In your kitchen so many afternoons,
in your last apartment, in this apartment.
This November afternoon.

←

Almost forty, childless,
so much of your life
given to ghosts. You lived with your story
longer than they were stranded
on that boat, on the verge of war.
Longer than the war.
Years later, you pushed the manuscript across the table
without comment. Your daughter almost as old
as the abandoned pages.

In a dream
the hooded hawk is sometimes
love, sometimes
death; everything stops at the moment
of unmasking.

Colette said, when one we love dies
there's no reason to stop
writing them letters.

Since you died,
love has opened every place
that won't open.

In a dream you said,
I am being reborn in
the womb of the earth.

You were with them,
those without place.

In your last apartment,
early winter
late afternoon.

Your face had the tenderness
of a hand.

III

FONTANELLES

"How much must be forgotten, out of love,
how much must be forgiven, even love."
— W. H. Auden, "Canzone"

Chalk and beeches. The winter sea
looks for itself in the new dark,
turning the smallest colour.

We brought our daughter here
before she was mortal. Before I knew
a person can be a prayer. Before
I had ever bathed a child, before
I felt another's death
could be my own.

We've gone on, each year
a little deeper, to the place
where land is geology, where objects are defined
by the space in them.
Where proteins assemble themselves
into souls. We've come in winter,
in the rain. To islands, to the abbey, always
cold, always looking,
to remember. Photographing the ruins

near Roan Fell. At North Beach and
Melmerby Fell. All the places where the earth
crumbles into edges.
The landscapes we saw
from love. From love,
to a marram field roaring under two thousand
Atlantic miles of moonlight, scent scoured
in the salt, as if an invisible woman
embraced us in the dark; the clover's
trace in cow's breath, in sweet milk,
woven by wind into the tall grass,
roots binding the sand. Arable islands
of porous lava, and islands so rigid the rain
bruises into peat, parietal
thumbprints in the gneiss
like the soft lakes
in an infant's skull.

Islands that are outer. Not barren
but precise. Not a wildflower
wasted.

The narrow channel, a gap of two thousand
million years. The inner basalt islands,
a green fifty million years old, where peacocks
fertilized lush gardens, darted
from massive hedges of rhododendron

while sugars and phosphates, thymine and
cytosine, guanine and adenine
aligned and divided with their three degrees of freedom;
in the winter, in the rain.

There is no song the sea
will not put in its mouth.

←

November mountains
the colour of marmalade,
mineral shadows. A thread of road clings
to the coast. Store, hotel, distillery.
The mysterious ways of the peat
can capsize a lorry like a toy;
the tides swallow a boat in seconds.
A glacial sea has nibbled caves and left behind
raised beaches, stranded high above the waves.
From Ardlussa, where the road ends,
seven miles through dense oak forest
to dying Orwell's farm,
the silent eyes of five thousand red deer
surrounding him in the night.

From Ardlussa, where the road ends.

←

Together we've looked to limestone and to apoptosis,
to discarded theories and the Abbés Glory and
Breuil, who followed children into the painted caves
of Altamira and Lascaux. To Jacques Loeb and
Jacques Monod, whose faith was biology,
who knew that awe is like an apple,
sweetest where the light collects,
under the skin. To everything
science breaks open to learn
what's inside, Irène Curie looking for truth
in a block of paraffin. To facts as unprovable
as one's own death. To icebergs
old as stone. To the granite sphinx
and the two-hundred-and-fifty-kilo priest
of Isis,
winched from the dusk
of Alexandria Harbour, from a sea bath
of sixteen hundred years.
And to how long
the handprint has marked the cave,
and to the nine months, and the time
twice that, for the fontanelles to close.

I've watched a woman swim
at North Beach, her pink belly

an eclipse rising from the waves; later,
the story she told, so close to me —
smell of coffee, rattle of ice, soft click
of billiards, through her Europe and her forests —
eager to speak before love made her
forget
where to begin. Long before
the first twenty cells, before
the corpus luteum, before
the microscopic heart,
long before hands and eyes.

I returned to North Beach and to
her words, the lake
winter-empty, tide trailing a branch
along the sand, while neural folds
fused. Before the brain, before gills
became bones or ears; "the ancient
genetic information shared with the fishes."

The distance a child travels,
tens of thousands of years,
one cell at a time. Cells that know
how to heal a wound from seam to seam,
from the depth. Cells that know
to assemble or re-
assemble themselves.

To regenerate blood and skin,
like a starfish that loses its arms
and grows them back again.

The body is a memory palace;
like Simonides' "inner writing,"
where each detail of each room corresponds
to one of the ninety-seven hundred lines
of Virgil's *Aeneid,*
or like tribes who use the whole Sahara
to remember a story.

Entropic catalogue.

The primitive streak, the blood islands.
Blessed protein.

    ↲

We came to photograph night. At the cliff,
to blacken film with the last atoms
of day. Later we'll look with faces
almost to the paper to see the waves,
creases of shadow darker than the dark
unlocking. Recall our

invisibility,
but for our white
breath.

A task, this waiting
for the dark, the slow disintegration
of sunlight, impossible to record
the moment one overtakes the other,
as it is to name the moment embryo
becomes foetus; the only time of day
quantum theory seems reasonable. When sight
is feeling. I think of Heisenberg's twilight
walks in Faelled Park, determined
to rid the universe of waves,
holding his head, minding terribly
his p's and q's. Or walking Copenhagen's
Langelinie, watching a freighter "fabulous
and unreal in the bright blue dusk . . .
biological laws exerting their powers
not merely on protein molecules but
on steel and electric currents . . ."
Or at four a.m. on the roof reading
Plato's *Timaeus*, neither
day nor night, the moment he knew
"that the smallest particles of matter
must reduce to a mathematical form."

Like sacred sites built from secular
stones — the priory filched from Hadrian's Wall,
or the Cistercian monastery built around pagan
altars to Jupiter and Silvanus —
spirit snags in the quantum mechanism.
Daughter cells, organelles, morula.
The shape of the belly
becomes the shape of the head.
From Ardlussa to North Beach.
From stones to atoms.
From atoms to stones.

The chemistry of looking;
to look until the river
swallows us, until the redness
of the stone fills our veins.
To look until we're
seen. But this is only longing.
We leave our heat shadows
in moss shocked with frost.
Even your camera
sees more; the detail you crave.
We strain to see even
what the camera sees,
what the eye can't; and this is as good
as a philosophy. An embrace
of failure, as if

just once, impossibly,
we'll catch the visible reflection
of what's invisible.
Our white breath in the dark.

How to photograph this,
the dark when one has said
too much. The dark
of sudden feeling. Love's
darkness.

The sea, folded paper;
rain filling each crease.
A twist of bright salt,
a twist of foam.
Phosphene.

Dark with hope.

←

A winter Sunday.
On the surface,
pilgrims to limestone, the cavers lay,
the earth's breath in their hair,
the breath of profound darkness,
ten metres and thirty thousand

years. Headfirst,
they dove into the draught.

They shouted into a chamber
too deep for lamps to grasp,
a sweating mineral space
white as exposed film in the darkness.
They unfurled a black plastic path
across the glinting calcite floor;
so their progress wouldn't disturb
the scattered bones and teeth and
tracks of ancient animals.

Aurochs and mammoths in charcoal and ochre.
In the gallery of horses
they shouted without words,
their joy
unpronounceable.

Near their feet,
under the gaze of pensive horses,
the imprint of two hands.

They ascended into the clean
chill of the gorge, dusk,
fine cold starlight

crystallizing their breath.
Dazed, they could only descend again.
And again, into the smell of wet clay;
the third time through the passage,
almost midnight, at last
bringing one who wouldn't believe
without seeing it herself –
a caver's daughter.

"We had lost all track of time."

←

You carry your camera
under the earth.

Rain wounds the snow. Gashes of mud
blacken a path. We light the lamps
and dive. Your sixty trillion cells
and mine. In the caves of Aldène and
Fontanet, paleolithic children played
while their parents painted. Small knee
prints and footprints in the clay.
Thousands of years later, the children return:
Maria who found the bison
on Altamira's stone sky;

Marcel who followed his dog, Robot,
into the mouth of Lascaux.

After eight weeks, the hands.
A mouth without lips.

After twenty-five weeks, filaments
follow a trail of chemical
scent through the cortex,
wiring up ears and eyes.
After thirty weeks, quantum whispering:
thought.

←

Almost in deference
to geologic time,
it takes generations
to become an islander.
Only ghosts earn a place.

The wind scrubs the air so clear
even the most crowded heart
remembers all it loves.

←

We bathe our daughter,
a prayer for every part,
as if we were washing her
with song.
Fingers frail as blades of grass.
Her thousands of eggs,
already inside her.

←

To love as if we'd choose
even the grief.

←

All love is time travel.

Scoured shore, painted caves,
limestone gorges.
Plums and cold water in the desert.

The winter river. This far.

A Note on the Text

"The Second Search"

The Polish physicist Marie Sklodowska Curie (1867-1934) and her husband, the French physicist Pierre Curie, shared an intense and productive partnership, both in their marriage and in their professional lives. In 1903, they earned a Nobel Prize for Physics for their discovery of radium, together with the French scientist Henri Becquerel. When Pierre Curie died suddenly, in a traffic accident in Paris, Marie Curie began a private journal, "the grey notebooks," where she wrote out her grief.

"Ice House"

Kathleen Scott was a sculptor, and the wife of the Antarctic explorer Robert Falcon Scott. They had been married two years, with an eleven-month-old son, when Scott went south to the Pole. Upon parting in New Zealand, they made a pact to keep a daily journal for each other. Scott perished on the return journey from the Pole, and when his body and the bodies of his companions were found in the spring, his diary was brought back to England. On the inside cover, Scott had written "Send this diary to my wife." Then Scott drew a line through the word "wife" and wrote instead, "widow."

Acknowledgements

Thanks to the editors of the magazines and anthologies where versions of some of these poems first appeared: *Border Crossings, Event, Arc, Toronto Life, Windhorse Reader, Slow Dancer, Fish Drum, We Who Can Fly, Border Lines: Contemporary Poems in English.* "There Is No City that Does Not Dream" appeared as part of the Toronto Transit Commission's *Poetry on the Way* program.

The quotation on page 17 is from the poem "A Second Farewell at the Feng-chi Post-station" by Tu Fu, translated by David Hawkes in *A Little Primer of Tu Fu* (Hong Kong: Research Centre for Translation of the Chinese University of Hong Kong, Renditions Paperbacks). Copyright © 1987, 1994 by David Hawkes. Reprinted by permission of the publisher. The quotation on page 51 is from "Canzone" by W. H. Auden, found in *Collected Poems of W. H. Auden,* edited by Edward Mendelson (New York: Random House, Inc.). Copyright © 1976, 1991 by The Estate of W. H. Auden. Reprinted by permission of the publisher.

The quotations in "The Hooded Hawk" on pages 43-46 are from *Old Woman at Play* by Adele Wiseman. The quotation in "Fontanelles" on page 55 ("the ancient genetic information shared with the fishes") is from *Life Itself,* by Boyce Rensberger. The quotation on page 61 ("We had lost all track of time") is from *Dawn of Art* by Jean-Marie Chauvet, Eliette Deschamps, and Christian Hillaire. My thanks to these authors and to the authors of other books that were especially helpful in the research of various poems, including, for "The Second Search," *Marie Curie*, by Eve Curie, and for "Ice House," *A Great Task of Happiness*, by Louisa Young, from which the list of the *Terra Nova's* supplies were itemized.

Many thanks to Liz Calder.
Thanks to Becky Shaw and Katie Collins.

Thanks to Ellen Seligman. And to Heather Sangster. And to Anita Chong.
Thanks to Marilyn Biderman.
My thanks to Sam Solecki.
Thanks to David Laurence.
To T. F. & P. And to John.